# Christ
## *our morning star*

### THE ART AND INSPIRATION OF SIEGER KÖDER

Magdalen Lawler

BOOKS & MEDIA

First published in the United Kingdom in 2012
Pauline Books & Media
Slough SL3 6BS

Paintings © Sieger Köder:
*Schöpfung I, 2000*, page 8; *Maria.* Uracher Altar (Ausschnitt), page 15; *Heimsuchung*, page 22;
*Geburt Jesu.* Rosenberger Altar (Ausschnitt), page 27; *Jesus heilt Kranke*, page 32;
*Die Frau am Jakobsbrunnen*, page 36; *Sturm auf dem See*, page 40; *Petrus schrie: Herr rette mich*, page 45;
*Veronika.* Kreuzweg Rosenberg, page 51; *Jesus begegnet den weinenden Frauen.* Kreuzweg Bensberg, page 54;
*Jesus wird vom Kreuz abgenommen und in den Schoß seiner Mutter gelegt.*
Kreuzweg in der Kirche St. Stephanus zu Wasseralfingen, page 58;
*Der Gang zum Grab am Ostermorgen.* Wasseralfinger Altar (Ausschnitt), page 62;
*Verklärung,* page 69; *Maria von Magdala am Grab*, page 72; *Ostermorgen am See*, page 76

Graphic design MaryLouise Winters fsp

Scripture texts from the *Christian Community Bible*
© 1999 Bernardo Hurault, Claretian Publications
and *The New Testament, A Fresh Translation,* © Nicholas King, used with permission

Poetry from *Exsultet & All Will Be Well* music CDs by Tom McGuinness sj, pages 11, 28, 29, 47, 65,
used with permission

ISBN 9781904785613

**P**auline

BOOKS & MEDIA
Middle Green, Slough SL3 6BS – UK
0044 (0) 1753 577629
www.PaulineUK.org
email: orders@pauline-uk.org

*Pauline Books & Media is an expression of the ministry of the Daughters of St Paul,*
*an international Catholic community of religious women, dedicated to spreading the Good News of Jesus Christ.*
*In imitation of the Apostle Paul, who used every means to proclaim Christ, the sisters work with modern media*
*and technology for evangelisation.*

Printed in Italy by Arti Grafiche Cuneo S.r.l. - Cuneo

# Christ
## *our morning star*

May the Morning Star
which **never sets**
find this flame still burning:

**Christ** that Morning Star,
who came back from the dead,
and shed his **peaceful light**
on **all** humankind,
your Son,
who lives and reigns **forever** and **ever**.
**Amen!**

*Easter Exsultet*

*May the Morning Star which never sets, find this flame still burning here; Christ, our Morning Star who came back from the dead, to shed his peaceful light on humankind.*

*The Church's ancient hymn of Easter praise addresses Christ as the Morning Star. It refers to a natural phenomenon when the planet Venus appears in the east before sunrise, sometimes seeming to be the very sun itself, as it rises in the sky. This image of the morning star brings hope of a new day and a new dawn. The morning star sheds a peaceful and gentle light which heralds the sun's rays. In this image we see Christ, himself, first born of the Father, who brings his peace and hope to our darkened world. He shelters us from the rays of the sun and introduces us to the light in a gentle and tender manner through his simple birth of a mother chosen from our midst.*

*Sieger Köder, priest and painter, has offered us many beautiful images to show us that Christ is at the centre of our lives and that in his light we have no need to fear. We may approach God as the very children of God that we are; co-heirs with Christ himself (Rm 8:17).*

*This book opens with one of Sieger Köder's most beautiful images of creation. We see Christ as the fullness of God's creation and we accompany him on his journey into our world, to live as we do. By his death and resurrection he acts as a model and Saviour for us all. The passion of our planet is the passion of Christ himself 'and in his rising our hope of resurrection dawns' (Easter liturgy).*

*Sieger Köder uses images of Scriptures and daily life to show that we can find God in everything – if only we have eyes to see. We feel privileged to offer you this rich reflection on Fr Köder's paintings in an accessible format and we hope it will be a valuable resource for you as the Spirit continues to open your understanding of the Scriptures in the gentle radiance of Christ our Morning Star.*

*Pauline Books & Media UK*

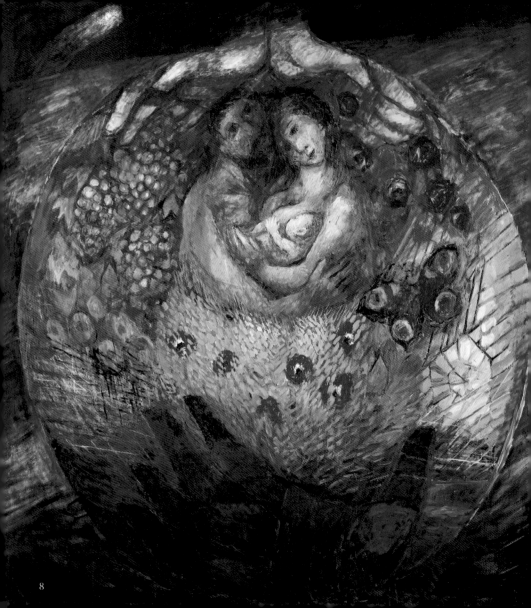

# in the beginning

●●

And God saw that it was good. *(Genesis 1:10)*

Cosmic dust clouds speed across this picture as we are drawn to reflect on the moment of God's creation.

Set in the darkest blue to evoke aeons of time and space and billions of light-years, as well as the womb, our planet emerges as a glowing sphere gently birthed into the cosmos. Our new star is taking its place in the harmony of the universe.

The generative hands of God open up to disclose the wondrous planet earth and all its riches, with humanity at its centre, placed there to enjoy the generous gift of Creation.

God's Spirit hovers, both as a dove and as a receptive hand, our world and our choices safely mothered in the shelter of its brooding wings.

Full of hope and fruitfulness, humanity is offered the perfection of Eden garden. Surrounded by fruits, flowers and grain, the nuclear family – a human trinity of mother, father, child – contemplates the goodness of God's Trinity through the variety and beauty of God's gifts.

To the right of the sphere caught, as it were, in a moment of time, the ephemeral and the enduring are suggested by the short-lived, delicate beauty of the butterfly and the strata of Jurassic fossilised rock. This crucible of civilisation draws our mind to the eternity of God. While all things have their time and their season, the hand of God embraces all.

Darkening chromatic edges to the picture suggest that despite all this loveliness, everything is

9

not at ease with our planet. The greening of our forests is under threat. The family and its future are no longer safe. The passion of the planet is suggested by the presence of Köder's signature red roses, a hallmark of his engagement with passion and suffering; often used by him in the context of suffering, war and want. Poppies, too, lend their memories of battle and strife between peoples.

But in the upper left distance of the picture plane, the bright Morning Star that never sets, speeds into our view *(cf Exsultet)*. Can this new star be the star of wonder perceived by the wise ones? Dare we hope that there is one more gift that God can offer to our world? Are we too presumptuous to suggest that there is One in whose hands the healing of the planet is safe?

The presence of a new Passion, evoked by the presence of the Eucharistic gifts, wheat and grapes, water to cleanse, draws us to a hope that God is about to give the most Beloved gift of all – God's own Son; God's beloved child; One of us, too. One who understands the groaning of our planet; One who suffers with us and is both enduring in his divinity and ephemeral, like us, in his humanity. Like us he will be born of a mother and live in a human family. As God he will rise again and bring humanity to the possibility of new life and new birth with him. His family will be from all times and nations and he will be named Jesus, Saviour.

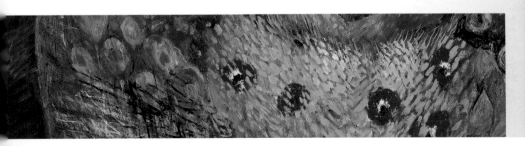

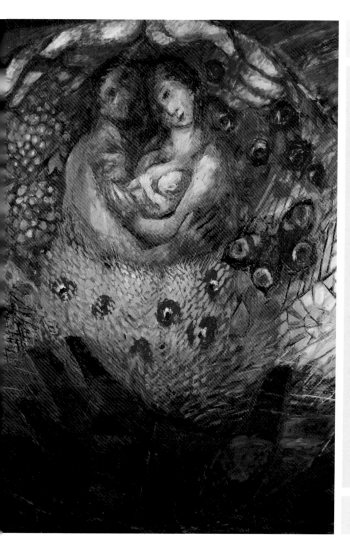

# We pray

O God,

we thank you

for the wonder

of your creation.

Move our hearts

to cherish our planet

and all its peoples.

May we receive

all your gifts

with respect

and with joyful thanks.

11

# *Lady so still*

Lady, so still, lost in the moment of your listening,
is it the soft wind or the Spirit gently singing?
Do you see the messenger who comes to call your name,
or is it just a movement in the air above a candle-flame?

Lady, so still,
    lost in the moment when your heart is full of praise,
    show us, in the coming days, the message that you hear:
    in your silence God is very near.

Lady, so still, lost in the moment of your answering,
is the curtain gently torn to open up your mind?
Can your soft blood run the risk of bearing us a child?

Lady, so still,
    lost in the moment when your heart is full of praise,
    show us, in the coming days, the message that you hear:
    in your answer God is very near.

Lady, so still, lost in the moment of your wondering,
form the Word that tears apart our darkness, lights the burning sun:
the life that has created us, the Power of the time to come.
The God of Love who holds our world forever in his hand
is no more than a murmur in your womb:
the Word is just a murmur in your womb.

Lady, so still,
    lost in the moment when your heart is full of praise,
    show us, in the coming days, the message that you bear:
    in your silence God is very near.

*Tom McGuinness, sj*

# handmaid of the Lord

●●

*Do not fear, Mary, for God has looked kindly on you.* (*Luke 1:30*)

Sieger Köder chooses contrasting colour temperatures to set this scene. The realm containing Mary and the Angel are in cool, cerulean blue, suggesting the night sky and the beauty of the stars. Mary is central to this picture and she occupies the central plane. Joseph is grounded in warm, earthy tones of brown and ochre. He lies in deep darkness, lit only by the light from Mary's hands, which reach out to him appealing to him for help, kneeling as she does, beside his bed, in his dream. Like his Hebrew namesake from the book of Genesis (*37-50*), Joseph is the one who shows us the power of dreams and that the dreams of our ancestors in the faith are about to be fulfilled.

Gabriel, the messenger of God, fills the night sky with a glimpse of the Presence (or *Shekinah*) of God, which will be poured out upon the shepherds at the birth of Mary's son, when they receive their own annunciation.

Hovering also between heaven and earth in her stillness, Mary raises her face to the Morning Star and closes her eyes to listen to God's desire for her, just as the angel has urged her to do. The child is to be seen enclosed in a sphere, evoking a new earth and a new cosmos, 'the bright Morning Star which never sets' (*cf Exsultet*). It is wonderfully reminiscent of the sacred disc in which Christ is often to be seen in eastern icons, enthroned upon the heart of Mary. Soon he will take up residence in her body and he will grow like any other child, dependent on her for life and warmth.

Cry out with joy, O daughter of Zion; rejoice, O people of Israel! Sing joyfully with all your heart, daughter of Jerusalem! …Do not be afraid nor let your hands tremble, for the LORD your God is within you, the LORD, a saving warrior (*Zp 3:14-15*).

# handmaid of the Lord

Hands are very eloquent in this painting. The hands of God and of Gabriel are large and powerful, but gentle too, and the sphere which contains the child has the insubstantial quality of an air bubble in its fragility – a fragility held gently in the hands of God. This vulnerability has its echo in the heart of Mary as she seeks to discover how this great truth can come about. But her hands are open to God's will for her.

How can this be if I am a virgin? *(Lk 1:34)*

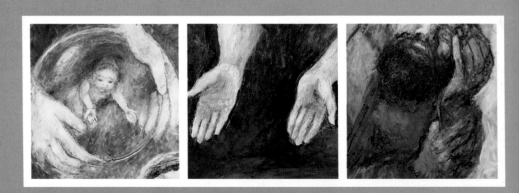

# We pray

God of love,

help us to contemplate

the heart of Mary

as it opens to receive

the gift of Emmanuel.

May we listen

to the peace

within her heart

and be ready

to open our own hands

and hearts

when we hear you call

our name.

18

# the annunciation
# to Joseph

Joseph, do not be afraid to take Mary as your wife. *(Matthew 1:20)*

Joseph's hopes are fragile, too. His plans are in turmoil and the Gospel of Matthew expresses this when we are told that Joseph is about to divorce Mary informally when the angel approaches him in his dream *(Mt 1:18-25)*. He adopts the classic posture of grief, cradling his head in his hands as he seeks a path through the maze of God's plan for him and for Mary, contrary as it is to their social and religious expectations. Like humanity, he slumbers in a long sleep of waiting, longing to be called back from the brink of unconsciousness to the fullness of life.

Like any human child, reaching for its mother, the child stretches out wounded hands towards Mary and towards humanity. In the billowing cloud and light, which accompany the Angel, the Holy Spirit is inferred. Mary is assured that 'the Holy Spirit will come upon you; and the power of the Most High will cover you with its shadow' *(Lk 1:35)*. The shadow is a direct reference to the cloud of God's presence *(Shekinah)* which accompanied the Hebrews through their desert escape from Egypt and their search for the land of promise, in the form of a cloud by day and fire by night *(Ex 13:21-22)*.

'Do not be afraid,' is the Angel's message to both Mary and Joseph. The presence of God is very often experienced with a frisson of fear, for the Angel tells Mary that 'the Holy Spirit will come upon you and the power of the Most High will overshadow you; therefore, the holy child to be born shall be called Son of God' *(Lk 1:35)*. But fear is driven out immediately by the reassuring message that God will accompany Mary in her call. 'Fear not, for I have redeemed you; I have called you by your name; you are mine' *(Is 43:1)*.

19

# the annunciation
## to Joseph

Mary's hands are stretched out and open to accept the message of God with a generous heart, as we know she does from the gospel passage. They also appear to be stretched out towards Joseph, pleading with him for shelter for herself and her child, but at the same time offering him a share in the wonder that is to be the family's destiny together. With her, we stretch out our hands to accept the wonder of Emmanuel: God with us.

# We pray

Call us back

from the brink

and bring us

to consciousness

of your presence

in our lives

when we don't know

who to turn to.

May we trust you

with the trust of Mary

and of Joseph

and be led forth

on our own journey

of faith.

# the greeting

**Blessed are you who believed that the Lord's promise would come true!**
*(Luke 1:45)*

Mary's visit to the home of Elizabeth is the springboard for a much deeper understanding of the Incarnation. It acts as a catalyst for Mary's dawning understanding of her role in the drama of God's plan and for her recognition of those whom her Son will save. Elizabeth will move us to a response that recognises Jesus as Lord for the first time in the gospel narrative, as she is the first to use this title for him. She also moves Mary to a response that recognises the justice and tenderness of God for all the poor and needy as she breaks into her song of the Magnificat *(Lk 1:46 ff)*.

Sieger Köder's painting is one of mystery. The simple reality of the shared experience of pregnancy is used to reveal the wonder of what is to come. The greeting between the two women takes place in a barren and arid landscape. Their sombre colours echo the surroundings of the desert which has been associated with the Baptist and with the exile of God's people. This may also be an attempt to remind us of Elizabeth's barrenness, a symbol of the barrenness of our world, which will soon spring to new life. As an adult, Jesus will submit to John's baptism in the Jordan waters. Then he will enter the desert, where he will be tempted.

Elizabeth kneels and places her head on Mary's breast, perhaps the better to hear her heartbeat and the heartbeat of the tiny life within her. She looks pale and drawn, as she reaches out to Mary, whilst Mary looks gentle and comforting towards this ageing woman whose desire for a child has but lately been fulfilled.

# the greeting

Elizabeth is a proud prophetess of the New Testament. We are told that she is filled with the Holy Spirit and cries out in a loud voice: a cry reminiscent of the cry before the Ark of God when it was carried into the midst of the Hebrews. The evangelist uses the same word for Elizabeth's cry of joy as the one that is used for the great shout of acclamation before the Ark. Mary is the Ark of God's presence now, and Elizabeth is the first to recognise this. She praises Mary for the belief she has shown in God's promise and Elizabeth's unborn child leaps in delight as the first meeting takes place between Jesus and his precursor, John the Baptist.

High above us, in a darkened blue and heavenly sphere, evoking the waters of their mothers' wombs, and the water of the river Jordan, the adult John and Jesus are palely etched as they recognise each other. John holds the shell of the Jordan baptism water and points to the Lamb whose sandal he is not worthy to remove. Jesus, with head bowed, and hands folded in prayer, prepares himself for the mission that is to be revealed in its fullness. Through the voice of the Father coming from the cloud and the presence of the Holy Spirit hovering over the waters, Jesus' own act of submission to John is transformed into a deeper understanding of his own mission and the beginning of the proclamation of God's reign *(Mt 3:13-17)*.

God's reign has already begun in Mary. In response to Elizabeth's greeting, Mary proclaims her great song of joy, the Magnificat. The framework for salvation is set out in its verses. Personal, social and political values are reversed and the atmosphere of God's kingdom is already revealed. Later we shall hear similar phrases as Jesus proclaims God's promises at the beginning of his ministry in the synagogue of Nazareth *(Lk 4:16-22)*.

# We pray

*O God of life,*

*we rejoice with Mary*

*and Elizabeth*

*at the birth*

*of their children.*

*Many children*

*enter this world*

*without the means*

*to sustain them.*

*Move us to work*

*for global justice*

*where the gifts*

*of earth are shared*

*more equally.*

# the nativity

••

As for Mary, she treasured all these messages
and pondered them in her heart. *(cf Luke 2:19)*

Cross beams rise up, as though from the hill of Calvary, in this tender painting of the Nativity of Jesus. The setting is the traditional one, portrayed by many artists. The action takes place in the stable and the Child is in a manger.

The bright Morning Star now sits in the sky and casts its light directly onto the Child. Like the shepherds and the magi, too, the sight of the star can fill us with delight as we ponder this wonder of our God made flesh.

At the centre of the picture the virgin-mother and Child draw us to their hearts. Mary is clothed in blue and the Child is wrapped in white to focus our attention and contemplation. Mary has stooped to lift her Child and she plants a tender kiss on his cheek. She leans in over the manger in a posture reminiscent of eastern icons, where Mary is often shown leaning into the crib from a recumbent position, having just given birth. She lifts the tiny child to her with tender eyes and loving hands. This child is the food of all creatures, the virgin-born grain of wheat, who will be crushed to become for us the bread of life. 'Unless the grain of wheat falls to the earth and dies, it remains alone; but if it dies, it produces much fruit' *(Jn 12:24)*.

The manger is inscribed with the proclamation, pinned at Pilate's command to the cross of Jesus: 'Jesus the Nazarene, King of the Jews' *(Jn 19:19)*.

# the nativity

Both the old and the new Law are shown at prayer before this solemn mystery; the prophet Isaiah in the foreground, predicting the virgin birth, surrounded by the flowers of the desert: 'Let the wilderness and the arid land rejoice, the desert be glad and blossom. Covered with flowers, it sings and shouts with joy…' *(Is 35:1-2)*. There is a child, too, who represents each one of us, leaning over the manger to gaze at this wonder with joy and delight. 'I assure you that unless you change and become like little children, you cannot enter the kingdom of heaven' *(Mt 18:3)*. This shepherd-child is come to greet the Shepherd-king and claim her promised inheritance of the Kingdom.

Perhaps we are being asked to suspend our expectations of who the Promised One might be, just as Joseph is being asked to suspend his expectations of Mary and her child. Joseph is portrayed in the classic eastern gesture of grief. This is a hard concept for the western mind to grasp, but in many eastern paintings it is the customary posture of Joseph at the Nativity. It serves to remind us of the struggle that Joseph had within himself, before he was able

to accept the message of the angel that came to him in his dream. What God was asking of him lay completely outside his social and cultural expectations. He appears to be still within that dream, as though, with humanity, he is being roused to wake up and see God's salvation, his true dream-destiny fulfilled. He rests his head on the hard wood of the cross, but he is shrouded in hope, symbolised by the green in which he is swathed.

We enter the stable with bated breath, looking around us, smelling the hay and the animals, but focusing on the child and his Mother, listening to their heartbeats in the imagination of our own hearts. We allow the Morning Star to cast its light into our hearts as we enter this joyful and profound mystery of hope for all humanity.

# We pray

*Help us to be aware*

*of the small joys*

*of our daily lives*

*so that we may recognise*

*the joyful song*

*of all creation*

*that your Son*

*has become one of us,*

*sharing our earthly joys*

*and sorrows too.*

*Glory to you,*

*O God,*

*and peace to all peoples.*

# Who but a God?

Who but a God could gather the cold winds,
folding the open air,
stretch out a light so clear? *(Job 38)*
Who but a God could open the old wounds,
call up our deepest fears,
only to offer the healing of his Word?

Who but a God would want to hear us?
Who but a God would want to hear our call?

Who but a God take boat on the calmest sea *(Luke 5)*
springing his kind words,
hung upon threads of air,
echoes of old songs for those who were hungry to hear?
Who but a God could offer the whole truth, *(John 6)*
loaves of a new bread,
potent with liquid words,
who but a God could offer himself as food?

Who but a God would want to feed us?
Who but a God would want to feed us all?

Who write so formless but with such intent, *(John 8)*
marking the dry sand,
holding only an openness of mind,
folding forgiveness around a lonely friend,
such love only a God could show.

Oh, who but a God could know the silent cry *(Luke 8)*
sharing so gently the Spirit's power,
calming a sudden fear,
healing a secret, carried for so many years?

Who but a God would want to heal us?
Who but a God would want to heal us all?

Who but a God could stand with such authority, *(Mark 14)*
facing the sad lies,
half-believed and hurled out in angry fear?
Who but a God could speak without saying a word?
Who but a God could face the final sin,
deep within the world he chose to share,
ah, who love so fully those placed in his care? *(John 17)*

Who but a God would want to free us?
Who but a God would want us as his own?
Only a God would come among us,
only a God would choose us as his home.

*Tom McGuinness, sj*

# healing life

**The Spirit of the Lord has been given to me, for he has anointed me.**
*(cf Isaiah 61:1; Luke 4:18)*

The bright morning star shines at the centre of this detailed painting, with the Easter promise of new life and themes that suggest discipleship and healing. Sieger Köder has chosen to make a contemplative collage of Jesus' ministry of healing. Within a numinous cloud of light, created from white and gold tones, reminiscent of the Transfiguration, Christ is portrayed in his divinity. He is surrounded by the many signs of healing that were a characteristic of his ministry. The golden tones are contrasted with blue and ochre as our eyes are drawn to the central image.

The main focus of this painting is the account of a young man whom Jesus raised from the dead *(Lk 7:11-17)*. The youth's mother has thrown herself at her son's bier as he is being carried to his burial. We are told by Luke that Jesus was at the gate of the city of Nain, with a great number of his followers, when the young man, the only son of his mother, was carried past, accompanied by many mourners. Aware that the woman was a widow, we are told that Jesus was moved with sorrow for her. We watch as divinity hides itself and the humanity of Jesus is displayed for us to see. 'Do

# healing life

not cry', Jesus says to the widow. Touching the bier of the dead man, Jesus addresses him, 'Young man, I tell you to get up.' We are told that the young man sat up and began to speak and Jesus gave him back to his mother. The evangelist intends us to see another Elisha at work here. 'A great prophet has appeared among us!' the people exclaim (*cf 2 K 4:8 ff*).

Sieger Köder has chosen this miracle as the central theme of the painting: the poignant moment when the mother falls before Jesus in awe and gratitude, and the bewildered son stretches out grateful hands towards his Saviour.

In the foreground there are fishing nets and boats abandoned on the shore, signifying the call of Jesus' earliest disciples from among fishermen on the Lake of Galilee. Peter kneels before his Lord as John looks on. Clearly visible is James, with his pilgrim's staff and scrip. Close to Jesus, Mary of Magdala seems to be the woman disciple who is witness to this miracle. Her portrayal is very similar to that by El Greco in the Descent of the Holy Spirit on the Disciples (*El Prado, Madrid*).

Wearing a white lacy mantilla she gazes at the Virgin Mary in that portrayal. In this, she gazes at her 'Rabbuni', as he draws the young man from death to life.

In the upper left of the picture plane, the paralytic throws away his bed; in the lower left a leper stretches out his hands for healing. The Scribes and Pharisees look on, probing and questioning. One is carrying the scroll of the Torah, another pointing to the new prophet who has appeared in their midst. The prophecy of Isaiah, read by Jesus in the synagogue at Nazareth at the beginning of his ministry is fulfilled in our midst. 'This text is being fulfilled today, even as you listen' (*Lk 4:16-21*).

We contemplate the gracious words and deeds of the incarnate Word.

# We pray

Let us feel

your gracious touch

as we bring before you

the needs of our hearts

and our world.

May we leave

our trivial cares behind

as you call us

to follow you

as your own disciples.

Bring us to new life

in your friendship.

# living water

●●

Sir, you have no bucket and the well is deep.
*(cf John 4:1-42)*

In this picture we are invited into the well of our own lives through the encounter between Jesus and the woman he meets at Jacob's well in Samaria. The well is a powerful symbol of life, especially in an arid land. It is also a matrimonial symbol because the patriarchs of Israel met their future brides at the well as they themselves watered their cattle and the younger women came to fill their water vessels. Rebecca and Rachel, matriarchs of Israel, were met in this way *(Gn 24:15-21; Gn 29:9-11)*. This was the only suitable contact between the sexes and subsequent marriage would need to be negotiated between the male members of a woman's household and the prospective husband.

The evangelist leaves us in no doubt about the connotations of the story. It follows Jesus' statement that the bride is only for the bridegroom. Jesus meets an unlikely bride of Israel at the well and she becomes the first apostle to the Samaritans, sharing with them the living water which he will give to them.

The picture invites us to gaze into the depth of the well of our own being with this unknown woman. She stands at the wellhead gazing into the water. She appears to be alone, both socially isolated, and alone in her contemplation. She also appears to be very young, at this stage in her contemplation, as though her life has yet to take its course. The well is exceedingly deep and dark, maybe symbolising her troubled life. She, however, is framed in the light of midday. Her meeting with the Sun is already implied.

# living water

Fierce light will be cast on her circumstances and, at times, she will flinch and change the subject in her ensuing conversation with Jesus. Whether she is a victim of Levirate marriage, with no choices of her own partners or, indeed, a woman of easy ways, we have no real means of knowing. What is clear is that Jesus knows her circumstances and she acknowledges this with the words, 'I see you are a prophet' *(Jn 4:19)*.

Their ensuing theological conversation is reflected in the water at the bottom of the well. God, worship and personal choices are all addressed in their exchange. At the noonday, when she senses she would be alone, this woman encounters the one who is the Living Water, who gives life to all beings as their Source. We see Jesus and the woman engaged in deep dialogue, as

reflections in the water. If we look closely we see that the woman appears older, as though she has matured through this encounter. The many rivulets that lie under the surface of her life have come together to form a spring welling up to eternal life, just as Jesus promises. The journey towards the well is one that she hitherto made alone. Now she is conscious that she is not alone in the events of her life, but rather that all the events have been leading her towards this meeting with the One who is. Her companions from the town no longer rely on her word because each of them has encountered Jesus and they are able to exclaim 'We no longer believe because of what you told us; for we have heard for ourselves and we know that this is the Saviour of the world' *(Jn 4:42)*.

# We pray

In your presence,

may we look fearlessly

at the events of our lives.

We know you are reflected

in the life of each of us

and that you offer us

living water to refresh us.

Move us to share

water resources

with all who suffer drought

throughout the world today.

# calming presence

Do not be afraid, for I have redeemed you;
when you pass through the waters, I will be with you.
(*Isaiah 43:1-2*)

Jesus got into the boat and his disciples followed him. Without warning a fierce storm hit the lake, with waves sweeping the boat. But Jesus was asleep. They woke him and cried, 'Lord save us! We are lost!' But Jesus answered, 'Why are you so afraid, you of little faith?' Then he stood up and ordered the wind and sea and it became completely calm.

The people were astonished. They said, 'What kind of man is he? Even the winds and the sea obey him' (*Mt 8:23-27*).

This picture is one of Sieger Köder's most dramatic paintings and carries us rapidly into the action on the Sea of Galilee described in the gospel. Both Matthew and Luke tell this miracle of the calming of the storm, with Jesus asleep in the boat. The prophecy of Isaiah develops our understanding of the story, as we see that it refers to each of us individually.

Strong blues and white dominate the scene and at the centre, we find a colourful group that draws our eyes into the picture. The boat itself seems to be tipped upwards, towards us, on the raging waters, inviting us to imagine that we too are present in the boat.

So we find ourselves in the boat in the roiling sea, alongside the disciples, while the storm rages round us. We hear the roar of the waves and the biting scream of the wind. We too are lashed by the salt water, so vivid is the picture. The evangelist and the artist conspire to draw us into the action and to imagine times when we have felt overwhelmed by events. We see the three men engaged in desperate action

41

# calming presence

to save the boat. Their heads are flung back at extreme angles in order to show the chaos that surrounds them.

Jesus is asleep in the stern of the boat, seemingly oblivious to what is happening. Sometimes we experience his presence as though he were asleep in our lives when we are most in need of him.

The contrast between the huge, arching shape of the waves, crested with white, engulfing the boat, and the jagged, futile action of the broken oars serves as a sharp reminder of the power of God and the frailty of humankind.

Each of us has experienced a time when we felt we were being engulfed by the circumstances of life. Jesus' message of calm is not an empty promise. His calming presence

is most effective when circumstances are least likely to promote peace and tranquillity. The peace of God's Spirit is not an easy peace but a robust peace – hard won and against the odds. Köder's boat is on the point of being capsized. It rides high on towering waves and is clearly beyond the control of the disciples, who desperately bale out and cry out to the sleeping figure of Jesus in their distress.

We may desire to shake our God awake when we find we can no longer deal with whatever life throws at us. 'Why are you so frightened?' Jesus asks us. 'Where is your faith?' Astonishment fills the hearts of his disciples. With them we ask ourselves who it is who can bring order from chaos and touch our lives with peace.

# We pray

*When you appear*

*to be absent*

*in our lives,*

*let us not fear*

*to wake you to come*

*to our rescue, Lord.*

*When we are*

*engulfed by life,*

*may we remember*

*your words,*

*'Why are you*

*so frightened?*

*Where is your faith?'*

# faith renewed

••

Lord! Save me! *(cf Matthew 14:30)*

Later in his gospel, Matthew, keen to emphasise the power and status of Jesus as Son of God, takes this miracle of the storm and develops it further *(Mt 14:22-33)*. He nurtures his infant Church of Antioch and leads us to an understanding of worship.

In this story the awesome power of water focuses our attention. Water can cleanse and heal, but it can also engulf and drown each one of us. This is a gripping tale and Sieger Köder paints it with great robustness of swirling, white crested waves and a bobbing, tilting boat. The disciples are once again on the Sea of Galilee. The incident occurs after the feeding of the crowd and Jesus tells his friends to cross the lake without him while he climbs the hills by himself to spend time in prayer and communion with God.

In the third watch of the night the sailors encounter a head-wind and once again their boat is close to capsizing on this capricious inland sea. The artist shows

us three of the disciples crouching in the doomed boat, its sail torn and flapping in the gale. Their pale faces are transfixed by fear of the storm. We are also told they think they see a shifting vision, which they fear must be a ghost. Köder shows their crouching terror and we can almost hear their abject cries.

With characteristic robust courage, Peter is the one who draws us into the action. We are told that he recognises Jesus and steps out of the boat having asked to share in Jesus' dominance over the waters. Confident, he begins to walk towards his Master across storm-tossed waves, but suddenly his confidence is rocked. His fright helps us to realise how it is for each of us and for the Church itself when we seem to be submerged beneath the

# faith renewed

buffeting waves of life. He becomes unsure and he begins to sink, despite his desire to imitate Jesus and be with him. With the waters threatening to engulf him, we listen to his heartfelt cry of worship ring out, 'Lord, save me!' The powerful hand of Jesus fills the forefront of the picture plane. The hands of Peter grasp the hand of Jesus that is being offered to him as he begins to drown. The gospel tells us that he cried out and 'at once' Jesus held him. There is simply no time between his cry and the aid that comes to him in the form of Jesus' firm, supportive clasp. As they board the boat together, the wind drops. The Lord of creation brings peaceful harmony to the elements once again, just as he does to our troubled hearts. 'O why did you doubt me?' Jesus says to Peter. And the reaction of the disciples is to bow in awe once again, before the Son of God. So, too, our baptismal faith is renewed after submersion in the waters and we are invited to unite in worshipping the Risen One who is always with his Church.

# We pray

Surround us with

your strength,

O God,

Creator, Son and Spirit.

Reach out to us

and grasp us to you.

Remind us too,

of the places in our world

where water threatens

to engulf the lives of many,

leading to death and disease.

May we plan a future

where all have access

to clean water.

# Yet I will

O my people, why do you want me dead
and clear of your minds, my people?
Why must I be torn from you,
forced from your once so welcome homes,
your welcoming hands?
Was it that I knew you too well,
understood too well your sad unsettled hearts
that you prepare for me a stark and lonely death?

Yet I will return, I will come back to you my people
to bring you where I am
to bring you home again.
I will return, I will not leave you long alone,
but I will bring you home
to my Father's side.
I will return and through the spirit that I send
I'll bring you where the darkest night can never fall again.

O my people, what have I done to you
that you cry out to have me killed, my people?
Was it that my words were just too hard to bear —
or that you would not hear them?
Was it that I loved you too well,
wanted only to bring fire to your hearts
and peace to your troubled lives,
that you forget me now,
that you reject me now?

Yet, I will return …

*Tom McGuinness, sj*

# true image

●●

We, with our unveiled faces,
reflecting like mirrors the brightness of the Lord. *(cf 2 Corinthians 3:18)*

This legendary woman, Veronica, whose name means 'true image', is privileged to reveal Jesus as the very veil of the Temple itself.

Her story, enshrined in the western Christian Church, is that an unknown woman in the crowd wiped sweat and blood from the face of Jesus as he travelled the road to Calvary. Her compassionate gesture caused the face of Jesus to be imprinted on her veil. The event has passed into Christian tradition and it becomes for us a moment when the veil of God is swept aside and the face of God is clearly seen, through the humanity of Jesus in all his suffering. Until this moment, the sight of the face of God was something to be feared *(cf Ex 3:6)*. Yet here our God is one of the least of humankind, and is accessible to each of us in our own suffering. Far from fear, our God evokes compassion from us – a compassion that reflects the very nature of God's own self. The starkness of the words of the prophet Isaiah rings in our ears: 'with nothing attractive in his appearance, no beauty, no majesty…' *(cf Is 53:2-5)*.

Veronica emerges from the darkness: only her hands and her eyes are visible in this picture. On her veil we see the face of Jesus, imprinted there in all its stark poignancy. The image appears like a shield before her heart.

# true image

Jesus appears to hold an empty, cracked bowl, perhaps representing the dustbowl of Africa and the many other places on our planet where humanity suffers from a lack of the most basic human needs: water, food, shelter and the means to live a healthy life and provide for one's family in peace. He shares that bowl with an unseen person whose hands reach out to us, crying out in their need – the stranger in our midst, the refugee, the child without hope of survival.

Veronica is wearing a mourning veil, covering her eyes, and she has offered her outer veil in this unique gesture of compassion. Her care calls us to a following of Jesus in which his image will be imprinted on our own hearts as Paul perceived in his letter to the Church at Corinth. 'The Lord is spirit, and where the Spirit of the Lord is, there is freedom. So, with unveiled faces, we all reflect the glory of the Lord, as though in a mirror, while we are transformed into his likeness and experience his Glory more and more by the action of the Lord who is spirit' *(2 Cor 3:17-18)*.

We ask to see the unveiled face of God as Moses did, and we ask that our own masks may be peeled away and that our inner faces, reflecting the face of Jesus, be revealed for all to see.

# We pray

Make us

into your true likeness,

O Lord,

as your image grows daily

within us.

May we see your face

in the needy and helpless

and respond

with compassion

to suffering

as did Veronica.

# journey with him

Women of Jerusalem, do not weep for me,
weep rather for yourselves and for your children. *(Luke 23:28)*

As Jesus travelled the road to Golgotha, bearing his own cross, he encountered a group of women whose hearts were wrenched with pity for him. It is Luke who preserves for us this poignant moment on the journey. Mourning and lamenting, as Luke describes, we see their upturned faces, though we do not see the face of Jesus; we can only imagine it.

The artist places Jesus at the dominant centre ground of his picture, bearing the heavy cross beam. His bent back, clothed in the scarlet seamless garment, and his upraised arms form a cross-shape in themselves. Our eyes are drawn to his broad strength and his bent posture towards the women. From his vantage-point he looks down on their group.

They may well have included those women that Jesus encountered in his public life: the bent woman, the woman at the well of Samaria, the haemorrhaging woman and many more. We cannot imagine that they had no more interest in him after their encounter with him. They gather round him, symbols of women of all nations and all generations, crying out in their pain, which is his pain too.

In the distance, barbed wire cries out their anguish and it forms a boundary to freedoms that are snatched away in our world today.

The sun is already beginning to be obscured in the sky and gathering darkness surrounds us as we enter the scene. We pay attention to his words, 'Happy are the women without child.' We have only to look at our world to realise that his words are truth in our own time. Across the globe we see women and children suffering the effects of war, famine and drought. The new slavery of trafficking women and children sits as a condemnation of our age.

We wonder at Jesus' ability to provide comfort at his darkest hour, and we ask him to be with us as we seek to comfort those who cry out for our comfort and practical assistance today.

# We pray

Jesus, you chose to reveal

to some women-disciples

the deepest truths

about your mission

to build the reign of God.

Women and children

are often at the bottom

of people's priorities.

May we give them all

the dignity they deserve

as beloved by you.

# a mother's love

••

To what can I compare you, O daughter of Jerusalem?
Who can save or comfort you, O virgin daughter of Zion?
Deep as the sea is your affliction, and who can possibly heal you?
*(Lamentations 2:13)*

It is a youthful mother who holds her son in her arms this final time before burial, as if she is re-visiting the moment of his birth. Swathed in the green of new life, Mary holds her son to her heart. With his head he nestles her cheek and shoulder as he did in his childhood. She who gave him life now presents him to us – his naked and blood-stained body like that of a child emerging into the world. Her first sight of him as he broke forth from her womb is also her last sight before he springs forth from the womb of God, bringing us with him as heirs. The mystery of Alpha and Omega is played out before us. Mary's child is born into new life and we are re-born with him.

Sieger Köder chooses sombre shades for this painting, but in the background there appears to be a dawning light, to represent the mystery of a new daybreak. The dove of hope and peace perches on Mary's shoulder and offers the olive branch of reconciliation for all humankind. At the place of the skull, Golgotha, our first parents, Adam and Eve, witness the event. Soon they will be called from their sleep; 'Awake O sleepers! Rise from the dead and Christ will give you life!' *(Ancient homily for Holy Saturday)*.

At this place of death, represented by the skulls of Eve and Adam and many more, the new Eve's task is accomplished with that of her Son. New life is beginning

# a mother's love

to dawn in the background and Easter day is already on the horizon. Mary will relinquish her Son to the tomb, but God will raise him up.

Mary is the archetype of all who are bereaved and who have lost loved ones. The loss of the beloved is when our faith is most challenged. With Mary we pray for the faith that we need to remain steadfast in the face of grief and loss and to recognise the accomplishment of a life lived in God.

# We pray

*We ask you*

*to bring into*

*your presence*

*all our loved ones*

*who have departed,*

*O Lord.*

*We ask your mother*

*to console us in*

*our time of grief.*

*May our faith*

*be strengthened*

*by the grace of her*

*prayerful compassion.*

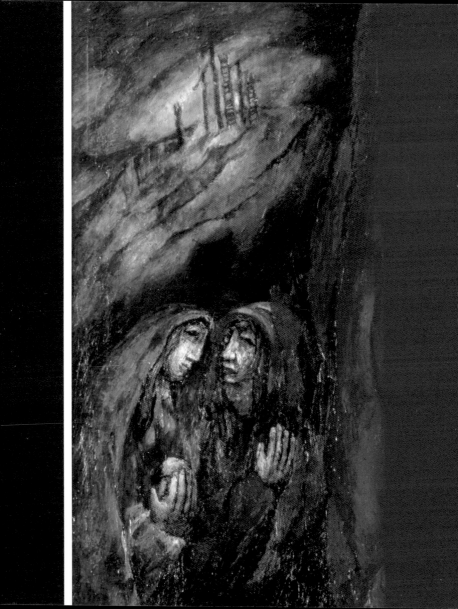

# gospel women

The women who had come with Jesus from Galilee
followed Joseph to see the tomb and how his body was being placed.
And returning home, they prepared perfumes and ointments.

*(Luke 23:55-56)*

In Mark's account of the passion and death of Jesus, the gospel writer draws our attention to a group of women-disciples. We are told, 'There were also some women watching from a distance; among them were Mary of Magdala, Mary the mother of James the younger and Joset and Salome, who had followed Jesus when he was in Galilee and ministered to his needs. There were also many others who had come up with him to Jerusalem' *(Mk 15:40-41)*.

Three significant verbs are employed by the evangelist to describe these gospel women, placing them in close personal attachment to the person of Jesus. Following always signifies discipleship. To look after Jesus is the same verb as to minister to him, which is the hallmark

of true discipleship. Coming up to Jerusalem always means to identify with Jesus in the Paschal mystery of his death and resurrection. The women tended to the needs of Jesus in life; now they seek to tend him in death by anointing his body for burial.

Sieger Köder captures the moment when some of those women descended from the Place of the Skull and accompanied the Mother of Jesus to the tomb. Their grief is tangible and the artist paints it in broad strokes using sombre shades of blue, purple and red. Huddled together they lean into one another for support. One clasps the ointment jar and the other gestures towards her heart. As they make their descent, tears course down their faces

# gospel women

and in the background the wind howls and rivulets of rain course down the hill of Calvary. The wind seems to draw them into its vortex as they drag their footsteps in sorrowful procession to the place of burial.

This picture is the embodiment of their grief. Desolation is tangible and we see their like in every corner of our world today where women and their children suffer through war, famine and exploitation. Our consciousness is stirred by their need, and their hands and eyes reach out to us in their own suffering.

We ask those women at the Cross to step apart and invite us into their company. With them beside us we can trust again in the One who will soon bring them and us to new life.

Light can be glimpsed among the crosses on the hill. We await the dawn.

# We pray

*Jesus, it is our privilege*

*to stand in the company*

*of these women*

*at the foot of your Cross.*

*We know your Cross*

*is the means*

*of our salvation.*

*Help us to bear the cross*

*in faith and love of you*

*and of our world*

*that you have saved.*

And the morning will be blessed

## And the morning will be blessed,

even when the darkness comes riding in …
hovering on beating wings …
cutting back the light … whispering of endless night …
even when the emptiness of deafness rings …
nothing can be felt or sensed,
nothing shows the strangest guest
who promises the morning will be

## blessed with light … blessed with the open sky …

blessed with cold, holy, clear and cleansing the morning cloud …
golden the feet, so firmly on the ground.
Gracious in meeting and spoken word …
knowing the limits and freedom that truth can share.
Lovely in laughter and knowing grief …
curtained in clarity, still in transparent belief …
blessed in the morning and blessed over and over all …
listening well to the inmost call
of the One, Open, Holy and Most Alone
calling his christed and chosen ones,
stooping to hold in the storm times …
leaving us free to walk to him over the open sea:
calling us always to him alone,
– calling us always home.

## And the morning will be blessed,

even when the darkness comes riding in …
hovering on beating wings …
cutting back the light … whispering of endless night …
even when the emptiness of deafness rings …
nothing can be felt or sensed,
nothing shows the strangest guest
who promises the morning will be blessed!

*Tom McGuinness, sj*

# transforming light

••

Your God will be your glory. *(Isaiah 60:19)*

'And suddenly, as they looked around, they no longer saw anyone but Jesus only' *(Mk 9:8)*.

The artist divides the picture plane into two clearly defined realms in order to convey to us the profound mystery that is the Transfiguration. He draws a distinction between the essence of God, which is unknowable, and the human realm in which Jesus resides in his human nature. The upper area resembles the sun at noonday emerging on the mountaintop. The lower realm is painted in earth colours enhanced with brilliant green and touches of red.

Ascending Mount Tabor Jesus communes with God. Peter, James and John have a momentary glimpse of the divine nature of their beloved master and so, too, a foretaste that all of created reality will be transformed through the resurrection of Jesus.

Köder solves the challenge of portraying everlasting light in the way that so many artists have solved it before him. His realm of light is in sharp contrast with the human realm at the bottom of the picture. He even draws a defining line to separate the two. The artist uses a golden and white haze to show Jesus, our Morning Star, emanating radiant light from his very person. Moses and Elijah are present with him, representing and affirming the Torah and the Prophets as they, too, are drawn into the light of the glory of God.

Radiance is the hallmark of this experience and this is evident in the expressions of all the characters. Their faces are transformed by what they perceive: the disciples with closed eyes, Moses and Elijah with bent bodies and praying hands. We too adopt this attitude of worship before this mystery.

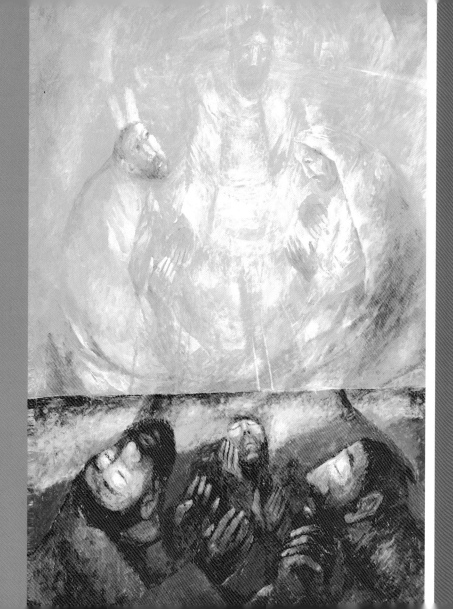

# transforming light

The mountain has come to be the symbol of transcendent experience throughout the history of our race. Jesus ascends Tabor with his earthly companions and they are invited into his mystery of transformation, with the promise that all of humanity will be thus transformed. Moses and Elijah ascended Sinai and Carmel where each of them encountered God in a profound way; Moses entering the cloud of God's presence *(Ex 24:16-18)* and Elijah finding God in sheer silence *(1 Kings 19:9-13)*.

In the lower segment of the painting, Peter voices the hopes and dreams of us all: 'Let us make three tents …' Like the disciples we can often long to remain in the transforming knowledge that our God is with us in a comforting way. But suddenly the disciples find themselves in the very presence of God's own self as the bright cloud draws them in and covers them too. They react as human beings react to the awareness of God's presence. We are told that they are overcome with fear, and cast themselves down onto the ground as if under attack. However, at the touch of Jesus, fear is again set aside. When they raise their eyes they see no one but Jesus only, in his human familiar self, his radiance concealed once again until his resurrection. He is truly God with them and with us.

'This is my Son, the Beloved, listen to him' *(Mk 9:7)*.

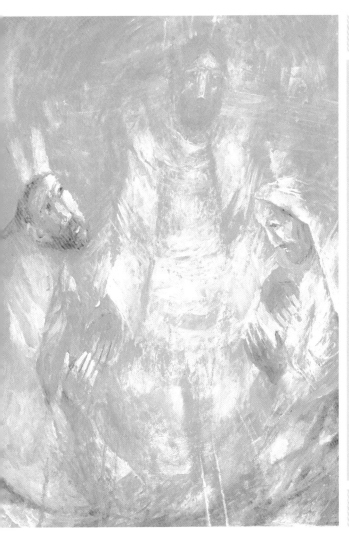

# We pray

We believe in your
transforming presence
with us, O Lord.

Help us to be light
wherever we
encounter darkness.

Make our relationships
and actions
beacons of your light
so that all may know
that we are your disciples.

# Rabbuni!

●●

*I looked for him whom my heart loves,*
*I sought him without finding him.* (*Song of Songs 3:1*)

John sets the scene for us: 'Now, on the first day after the Sabbath, Mary of Magdala came to the tomb early in the morning, while it was still dark and she saw that the stone blocking the tomb had been moved away' (*Jn 20:1*).

Dawn breaks in the distance, in this painting by Sieger Köder. He chooses to focus on the tradition in John's gospel that Mary of Magdala came first and alone to the tomb on Easter morning. Mary is shown in the garden of Jesus' burial, surrounded by tombs and the symbols of death. She is clothed in brilliant red, which echoes the dawn. Our eye is drawn to her central position and kneeling posture. She is just turning in recognition of the risen One. A wall encloses the place of burial, like the walls we construct to keep others out and ourselves within.

We are reminded that it was 'very early in the morning and still dark' when Mary of Magdala came to the tomb. These words cast our consciousness back to the dawning of time, and the first day of Creation. The artist helps to set the stage for the resurrection and a new creation. In the distance the rising light of dawn seems to have pierced the wall and set it asunder. We wait for the moment when Jesus will emerge from the tomb to newness of life.

Mary is closely associated with the Song of Songs. From the fifth century onwards, at Ephesus and elsewhere, it has been the chosen reading for her feast. She is depicted as the one who constantly seeks the Beloved: 'I looked for the one I love, I sought him without finding him; I called him and he did not answer. I will rise and go about the city,

# Rabbuni!

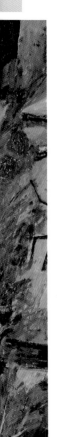

through the streets and the squares; I will seek him whom my heart loves …' *(Sg 3:1-3)*.

So Mary is shown touching the stone where the tomb is inscribed 'Jesus of Nazareth' as though this contact will help her to find him. She searches, longing to anoint him with the spices she has lovingly prepared. When she peers into the tomb, she sees two angels sitting where the body of Jesus had been; like the cherubim of the Ark flanking the Mercy Seat *(cf Ex 25:17-22)*. The angels ask her, 'Woman, why are you weeping?' Jesus will ask her the same question when she meets him in the garden. Bewildered, she turns and in this moment of conversion her perception of everything is completely turned and re-aligned. Hear him ask us too, 'Humanity, who are you really seeking?' Mary recognises Jesus at the sound of her own name, 'Mary'. She responds in the fullness of love and faith: 'Rabbuni!' *(cf Jn 20)*.

The breaking dawn is the source of natural light in the background but greater light lies in the foreground, beyond our vision. Our Morning Star has risen again. Mary is clearly lit by the glory of the resurrected One. She will experience the deepest mystery of Christian belief and her radiant red garment shows us the joy she will experience. All at once, there was a violent earthquake *(cf Mt 28:2)*. The walls of death are shattered; great fissures appear in the tombs. The guards are now like the dead. Life has vanquished death.

The artist moves our focus to Mary's feet, turned towards us in their vulnerability. Mary's apostolic commission is conferred; hers are also the beautiful feet that bring the gospel of peace. Jesus' message to her is: 'Go, find my disciples and tell them … I am ascending to my Father and your father, to my God and your God'. So Mary of Magdala comes, announcing, 'I have seen the Lord!' *(Jn 20:18 – Translation by Nicholas King sj)*.

# We pray

May we seek you

with the dedication

and perseverance

of Mary of Magdala

and find you

in the unexpected events

of our lives.

May we follow

her example and share

her witness

with our world

as we join her

in proclaiming

your resurrection.

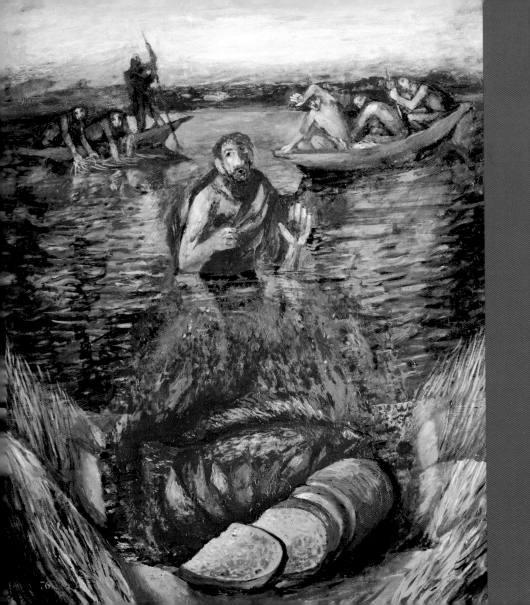

# It is the Lord!

●●

Jesus appears to Simon and the other disciples by the lakeshore.

*(cf John 21)*

The artist draws our eye towards the charcoal fire at the centre front of this picture. We are immediately reminded of the burnt sacrifice of the Covenant with God's people, where the firebrand signified the Lord, the God of Abraham *(Gn 15:17)*. Here the gospel describes the inauguration of a new Covenant in the blood of Jesus. The fish, in Greek, ICHTHUS, the cryptogram for the name of Jesus (the letters stand for Jesus, Christ, God, Son, Saviour), takes centre-stage in this reflection of forgiveness and reconciliation. Brilliant hues set the scene of resurrection: all the colours of the palette are on display, but the blood-red of sacrifice dominates. Peter emerges from baptismal waters, washed clean in the blood of the Lamb.

This episode at the end of the Gospel of John was probably added later than the rest of the gospel in order to affirm Peter and to reinstate him for leadership in the earliest Church. It reads like an action-replay of the life of Simon Peter. As we read it, we may wish to apply a similar 'action-replay' to our own lives, looking back to see where Jesus has accompanied us throughout life, though we were not aware of it at the time.

We are told, 'It was light by now when Jesus was standing on the shore, but the disciples did not know that it was Jesus' *(Jn 21:4)*. The Morning Star has returned and is not dimmed by the light of dawn. In this light – the light of the Risen Christ – Peter will see his whole life transformed and reconstructed.

# It is the Lord!

We see in the background a re-enactment of the miraculous catch of fish, nets spread wide. It reminds us and the disciples that Jesus drew Peter to himself to become a 'fisher of souls'. In the disciples shading their eyes from the vision of Jesus, we are reminded of the One who was transfigured before their eyes, the One who also calmed the storm and who called Peter across the shifting waves. Now Peter plunges more humbly into the water, wading to where Jesus awaits him. The gospel narrative reminds us of Peter's threefold denial of Jesus when challenged by a young servant girl. Now Jesus will nourish him with his own food as the crowd was nourished by the meal of loaves and fishes. Jesus will ask Peter to re-commit to him through an admission of sorrow and love. Jesus will commission him again in a threefold manner, to be not a fisher, but a shepherd of souls like himself.

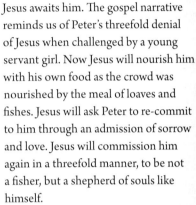

Love is the hallmark of this gospel passage. Like the burnt sacrifice, Peter will be assayed in the furnace of Jesus' love. He will emerge as gold and he will be able to respond with heartfelt faith and joy, 'Lord, you know everything; you know that I love you' (*Jn 21:16*).

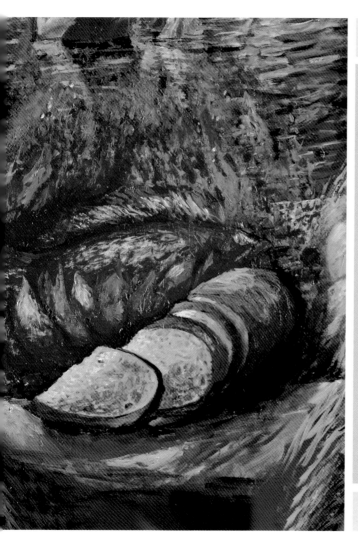

# We pray

Our lives are yours,

O Lord.

May we see them

in the light

of your gracious presence.

Even our faults

are transformed

by the hallmark

of your love.

'Lord you know everything.

You know we love you.'

# Sieger Köder

Sieger Köder was born on 3 January 1925 in Wasseralfingen, Germany, where he also completed his high school studies. During the Second World War, Sieger Köder was sent to France as a front line soldier where he was made a prisoner of war in 1944-45. Once freed, Köder studied engraving and silversmithing. He attended the Academy School of Art in Stuttgart until 1951 and then studied English philology at the University of Tübingen as part of his qualification as a teacher.

After 12 years of teaching art and working as an artist, Köder undertook theological studies for the priesthood, and in 1971 he was ordained a Catholic priest. From 1975 to 1995, Fr Köder was a parish priest in Hohenberg and in Rosenberg. He then retired to Ellwangen, not far from Stuttgart, where he now lives.

The years of Köder's parish ministry are among the most prolific with inspiring works of art. There is complete synergy between Fr Köder being a minister and an artist. He uses his paintings as Jesus used his parables. He reveals the depth of the Christian message through metaphors and by shedding light and colour on human history. Thus we understand why Köder's art is heavily charged with the experience of the Nazi period and the time of the Holocaust.

Köder's paintings are also rich with theological insight. He shows a certain reserve in representing the figure of Jesus, who most of the time is outside the scene. He seems to invite the viewer to look from Jesus' perspective in order to convey the idea that Jesus is alive today in the person of the viewer. Köder dips his brush into the very essence of the Gospel and with colour describes the wholeness of human life. Thus, his art is a vibrant glimpse of the depth, the length and the breadth of the mystery of Christ in each one of us.

The images of Sieger Köder's paintings are also available as posters, digital images, postcards and prayer cards. For complete information and for many more resources please visit our web site: *www.pauline-uk.org.*

## the author

Magdalen Lawler is a Sister of Notre Dame. After many years of work in secondary and tertiary education, Magdalen trained at St Beuno's in 1980 and was part of the retreat team at Loyola Hall, Merseyside, from 1980 to 1983. Since then she has worked in retreats and spiritual direction in tandem with student chaplaincy at Liverpool Hope University and at Heythrop College, University of London. Now retired, Magdalen offers retreats throughout the UK. She has a special interest in women's spirituality and in the relationship between spirituality and the visual arts.

She is the author of *Encountering Christ, Conversations with Women in John's Gospel* and *Contemplating Christmas* as well as *Pathways to God's Goodness; the spirituality of St Julie Billiart* obtainable from **www.sndden.org**.

# RESOURCES

## posters

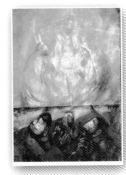

**Sieger Köder**

*Many of the images in this publication are available as posters and cards*

## music

**Exsultet & All Will Be Well**

*by Tom McGuinness sj*

*Music for the poetry in the four sections of this book is available on a double CD*

# THE ART AND INSPIRATION OF SIEGER KÖDER

## cd-rom

### Art and Inspiration

36 full-colour excellent
quality digital images

Includes the
Washing of Feet and
The Last Supper

## books

### The Folly of God

by Rina Risitano
18 images of the passion and
resurrection of Christ

### Glimpses of the Divine

by Gemma Simmonds

16 images from the Old and
New Testaments – prayerful
meditations for each painting